THE BARBADO

AND ITS BUILDINGS

Jill Sheppard

25 May 1980

Other Titles Published by the Authors:

Historic Bridgetown, Warren Alleyne (The Barbados National Trust, 1978)

The History of St. Patrick's Roman Catholic Cathedral, Barbados, Warren Alleyne, 1985

Caribbean Pirates, Warren Alleyne (Macmillan, 1986)

The Barbados–Carolina Connection, Warren Alleyne and Henry Fraser (Macmillan, 1988)

The Houses of the Barbados Assembly, Warren Alleyne (The Barbados National Trust, 1989)

The 'Redlegs' of Barbados–their Origins and History, Jill Sheppard (Kraus Thomson Press, 1977)

Marryshow of Grenada–an Introduction, Jill Sheppard (Published privately, 1987)

THE BARBADOS GARRISON
AND ITS BUILDINGS

Warren Alleyne and Jill Sheppard

Illustrated by David Jones

MACMILLAN
CARIBBEAN

First published 1990

Published by *Macmillan Publishers Ltd*
London and Basingstoke
*Associated companies and representatives in Accra,
Auckland, Delhi, Dublin, Gaborone, Hamburg, Harare,
Hong Kong, Kuala Lumpur, Lagos, Manzini, Melbourne,
Mexico City, Nairobi, New York, Singapore, Tokyo*

ISBN 0−333−52991−X

Printed in Hong Kong

A CIP catalogue record for this book is available from
the British Library.

CONTENTS

Foreword   vii

Introduction   1

Historical Background   7
  The First Fortifications in the Garrison Area
  (1650–1780)   7
  The Establishment of the Garrison (1780–1801)   11
  The Expansion of the Garrison (1802–1815)   14
  The Decline of the Garrison Including the Hurricane
  of 1831 (1816–1905)   18
  Life and Death in St. Ann's Garrison   21
  The Dissolution of the British Military Garrison
  (1905–1906)   28

Tours of the Garrison Historic Area   31
  Tour A: Area immediately surrounding the Savannah   32
  Tour B: Buildings within the perimeter of the Defence
  *   Force*   49
  Tour C: From Charles Fort to the Barrier Bridge   54

  Buildings outside the Garrison Historic Area   63

The National Cannon Collection   67

ACKNOWLEDGEMENTS

We would like to thank the following for granting us permission to use photographs:
The Garrison Committee for the water-colour sketch of the Main Guard by Arthur Pigott, the water-colour sketch of Carlisle Bay and Bridgetown by Arthur Pigott, the water-colour of St Ann's and the Barracks seen from the Savannah by C.M. Wilson, the aerial view of the Savannah, the photographs of the Cannon Collection and of the Cannon with the Cromwell Gun; the Barbados Museum for the print of the Brick Barracks in 1836 by Lieut. J.M. Carter, the oil painting of a Race Day on the Savannah by W.S. Hedges, the prints of St Ann's Garrison and the Savannah by W.H. Freeman; the National Library Service for the photographs of the Main Guard and of the Lock Hospital; Lady Chandler for the 'Dauntless' print of the Naval Dockyard; James Peck for the photograph of Cherry Tree Cottage; Peter Simpson for the photograph of the ladies receiving a trophy in front of the small guard house; and The Massachusetts Historical Society for the plan of St Ann's Fort.

FOREWORD

Brigadier R E C Lewis GCM, CVO, ED
Chief of Staff of The Barbados Defence Force,
Chairman of the Garrison Committee

This publication by Jill Sheppard and Warren Alleyne is timely. One of the tasks of the Garrison Committee since its inception has been to bring to public attention the importance of this historical area as part of the national heritage of Barbados. The restoration and preservation of its buildings are essential to this end and Jill Sheppard as Chairman of the Buildings Sub-Committee of the Garrison Committee has indeed focused attention on this aspect. Where praise is due she has given it and where she sees a threat looming she has been tireless in her efforts to bring this to the attention of the appropriate authorities.

Warren Alleyne has brought his vast reservoir of historical knowledge of Barbados to complement this production and we of the Garrison Committee are most grateful for his help and advice freely given, over these past years.

This publication is not only a factual catalogue of the historic buildings but it seeks to take the reader back in time to get the feel of Garrison life as it was lived. Captain Bunbury's letters do just this.

Finally I should like to emphasize that the Garrison, as its name implies, has always been associated with the military. It therefore gave me great pleasure as Chief of Staff of the Barbados Defence Force to have been asked by Government to be the Chairman of the Garrison Committee. Through our historic military connections I believe we have a responsibility to be involved in the preservation of this area as a memorial to those craftsmen and artisans who contributed to the construction of these fine buildings and to the soldiers who lived and served in them.

INTRODUCTION

The Barbados Garrison and its Buildings seeks to do two things. It seeks to provide an outline of the events of the past three centuries or so that led to the establishment, expansion, decline and eventual dissolution of the British Military Garrison in Barbados, and to give some idea of the life that was led by its denizens during those tumultuous years, punctuated as they were not only by wars in the region but also by large scale natural disasters in Barbados. It also seeks to enable the visitor to envisage something of the framework of that life by providing brief descriptions of the buildings that still exist – and of some that do not – and describing their changing functions over the years.

What this book does not presume to do is to provide a detailed, definitive history of the Garrison; that could indeed be achieved on the basis of the mass of information that is available in the Public Record Office (PRO) at Kew, near London, and elsewhere, but would require time and money – both of which are in rather short supply – and, in addition, the assurance of a serious interest in the subject on the part not only of military historians but also of a somewhat wider public.

Much of the information used does, in fact, emanate from the PRO, having been collected over the years by a number of enthusiasts; some comes from the records of the Barbados Department of Archives, some from the materials available at the Barbados Museum and Historical Society, and from articles in its Journal, some from the private collections and memories of those who themselves, or through their families and friends, have long connections with the Garrison. Acknowledgements are due to many people, who have helped in their various ways, and particularly to Peter Campbell, whose knowledge of the Garrison and the regiments once stationed there is probably unrivalled, and on whose knowledge and whose writings we have drawn unreservedly,

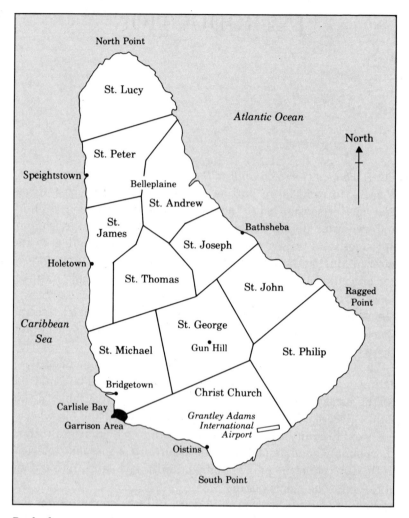

Barbados

and to Lady Chandler, who grew up in the Stone Barracks, in St. Ann's Fort, and whose childhood memories and current enthusiasm have been a great source of help and inspiration. Special mention also needs to be made of a number of volunteers who have helped over the collection and recording of information, specially Kate Woolverton and Sandra Stoddart, and Jean Blades, who has recently set up the basis of a Garrison Archive. Thanks are also due to Pearl Goodridge who, although faced by a number of problems, succeeded in completing the word-processing on schedule.

Reference should also be made to the Map of the 'Barbados Garrison Historic Area', originally published by the Garrison Committee in March 1986, and now, in a corrected and amended form, included in this book on pages 4 and 5. Extracts of this map have been enlarged and these should be consulted in conjunction with the section entitled 'Tours of the Garrison Historic Area', which attempts to bring the buildings of the Garrison out of their historical background, into the present and, perhaps, also to some extent into the future. In both sections of this book buildings are identified by the numbers used on the map. There is also included a note on the Cannon of Barbados, which are in the process of being assembled to form a national cannon collection.

For the Garrison has a future through, in part, the adaptive use of the buildings themselves, some of them, appropriately enough, by the Barbados Defence Force, but also through the attention that is now being paid to the preservation and enhancement of the area as a whole. While work has indeed been carried out on some of the buildings since the withdrawal of the British troops in 1905 and 1906 it is only comparatively recently that the matter has been approached with any degree of co-ordination. This has come about in the main through the activities of the Garrison Committee, which was set up in August 1983 and which, through the efforts of its members, and co-opted members, has been attempting, with some success, both to provide advice on the restoration of the buildings and the maintenance of the grounds and to make people generally more aware of the significance of the Garrison as a most important part of the historical and architectural heritage of Barbados and the Caribbean.

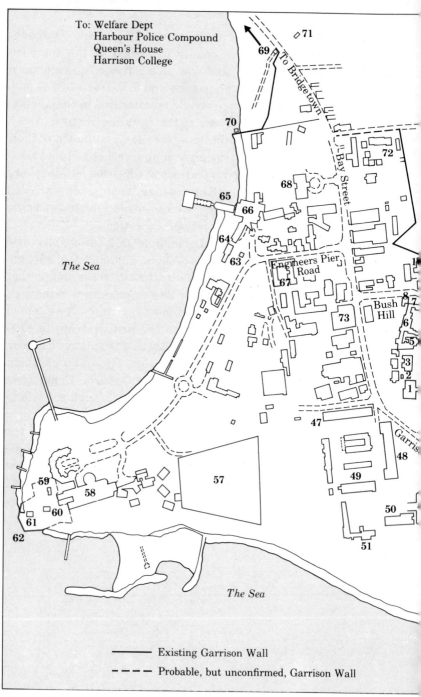

To: Welfare Dept
Harbour Police Compound
Queen's House
Harrison College

The Sea

The Sea

——— Existing Garrison Wall

– – – – Probable, but unconfirmed, Garrison Wall

Map of Garrison Historic Area
Based on map prepared by the Garrison Sub-Committee on Buildings,
drawn by David Sealy and Sandra Stoddart, and published by the
Garrison Committee in March 1986

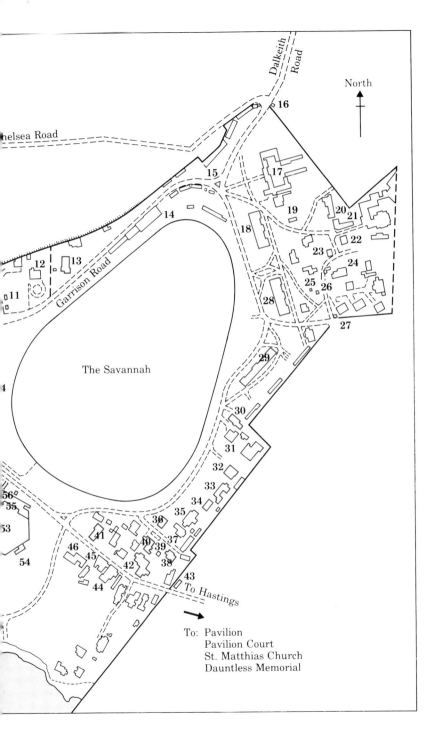

North

Dalkeith Road

helsea Road

16

15

17

14

19

20 21

18

22

23

24

12 13

25 26

Garrison Road

28

11

27

The Savannah

29

4

30

31

32

33

34

35

56

36

55

41

40

37

53

46 45

39

38

54

42

44

43

To Hastings

To: Pavilion
Pavilion Court
St. Matthias Church
Dauntless Memorial

HISTORICAL BACKGROUND

The First Fortifications in the Garrison Area (1650−1780)

The oldest building in the Garrison Historic Area, Needham's Fort, later renamed Charles Fort (59/60/61), dates back to about 1650, just 23 years after the English settlement of Barbados, at which time the Earl of Carlisle held the island as Lord Proprietor by grant from the King. It may seem strange that, in those troubled times, with the ever-present possibility of an attack from the Spaniards, little action was taken to fortify the island until developments in England brought this about.

With the end of the Civil War, the execution in 1649 of King Charles I, and the establishment of the Commonwealth under Oliver Cromwell, the skirmishing that had gone on in Barbados between Royalists or Cavaliers on the one hand, and Parliamentarians or Roundheads on the other, was brought to a head, with the former emerging triumphant. Thus it was only to be expected that action would be taken by Cromwell to reduce the island to submission to the Commonwealth. This had been foreseen by Lord Willoughby, who had obtained a lease of the proprietorship from the Earl of Carlisle and, having been appointed Governor by Charles II in exile, arrived in Barbados in early 1650 and set about strengthening the defences of the island. This included training and equipping the Militia, which had been set up in the 1640s and consisted of the majority of the freemen of the island, and providing them with arms and ammunition.

It was with the arrival of the Commonwealth expedition commanded by Sir George Ayscue in October 1651 that the first mention of the Fort at Needham's Point was made; the initial warning that a landing would be resisted came from the guns at the Fort as the ships entered Carlisle Bay.

Needham's Fort would not, at that time, have been constructed of stone but rather of fascines—bundles of saplings and branches—frequently used in those days for ramparts and other types of defences. Indeed, in 1656, when the Fort was undergoing repair, Governor Daniel Searle and his Council 'ordered that ye remainder of ye Mangrove trees growing near Needham's Point, and formerly bought for ye Country, be employed for to make piles for ye present repair of ye fort'. On the following 15 August the island's Treasurer was directed to pay each of the workmen employed on the Fort a monthly wage of 250 pounds of sugar—a commodity then generally used as currency—while the Gunner, the officer in charge, was in future to be paid an annual salary of 3000 pounds of sugar. It seems odd, at first glance, that these amounts should be the same; presumably the labourers worked full-time, while the Gunner, as a member of the Militia, would be on a part-time basis.

The name Charles Fort was substituted for Needham's apparently soon after King Charles II, exiled since 1651, had been restored to the throne in 1660. The Fort was without doubt the most powerful unit in the island's coastal defence system, mounting usually as many as 36 pieces of cannon. In April 1665, when a Dutch Fleet commanded by the distinguished Admiral Michel De Ruyter attacked Bridgetown, the guns of Charles Fort played an important part in repelling the invaders.

During Britain's wars with Spain (1739–1748) and France (1744–1748) two fascine batteries—one mounting eight guns and the other six—were constructed to guard the northern and southern flanks, respectively, of Charles Fort. A description of the Fort and its defences around the middle of the century was provided by the first President of the United States of America.

Major George Washington came to Barbados on 3 November 1751 as companion to his consumptive half-brother, Lawrence, who hoped to benefit from the warm, dry climate. The brothers rented a house on the site of what is now Bush Hill House (10/11) in the Garrison and during their residence, which ended on 22 December, they were entertained at Charles Fort (called Needham's by George Washington) on some four occasions by Captain Petrie, the officer in command. On Tuesday 13 November Major George Washington recorded in his diary: 'dined at the Fort with some Ladys; its pretty strongly fortified and mounts about 36 Gunes within the fortifin, by 2 fascine Batterys me. 51'.

PLAT OF QUEEN ANN'S FORT ON THE E SIDE OF CARLISLE BAY- BARBADOES

1709

NORTH SIDE OF THE DITCH

DITCH DUG IN YE ROCK 10 FOOT WIDE

DITCH DUG IN YE ROCK 10 FOOT WIDE

BRIDGY

GLACIS CUT ON YE ROCK

GLACIS CUT ON YE ROCK

DITCH DUG IN THE ROCK 10 FOOT WIDE

GLACIS CUT ON THE ROCK 18 OR 20 FOOT WIDE

3 LOOP-HOLES

3 LOOP-HOLES

4F 9 FOOT 6F

4F 9 FOOT 6F

FLOOR OF JOISTS

SIDE 18 OR 20 FOOT

SIDE 18 OR 20 FOOT

SIDE 18 OR 20 FOOT

SIDE 30 FOOT

MAGAZINE

SIDE 18 OR 20 FOOT

GLACIS CUT ON THE ROCK 18 OR 20 FOOT

SIDE 30 FOOT
GLACIS CUT ON THE ROCK
18 OR 20 FOOT BROAD.

DITCH DUG IN THE ROCK 10 FOOT WIDE

GLACIS CUT ON THE ROCK 18 OR 20 FOOT WIDE

DITCH DUG IN THE ROCK 10 FOOT WIDE

DITCH DUG IN THE ROCK 10 FOOT WIDE

BOUND ABOUT THIS FORT IS A PLAIN.
THE FORT ITSELF ON A HILL OF ROCK
THERE ARE BUT 6 CANNON THERE,
THE WORKS BEING VERY IMPERFECT.
YE BAY BATTERY LIES N6W ½ N.

Plan of St. Ann's Fort as it was in 1709

Around 1790 the south battery was dismantled; in 1811 the north battery was enlarged and improved, and then named in honour of Lieutenant-General Sir George Beckwith, Governor of Barbados and Commander-in-Chief of the British land forces in the Windwards and Leewards. Beckwith's Battery was still manned in the mid 1800s but was evidently in ruins by 1869. Also during 1811 and 1812 considerable reconstruction work was carried out at Charles Fort itself. All the old buildings were demolished, and some of their material used in the construction of the new ones, including a magazine.

With the outbreak of war with France in 1688 it had become clear that the defences of Barbados were totally inadequate and a military engineer, Talbot Edwards, was sent out to draw up plans for improving the fortifications. His concept, however, of a 'grand fortress and magazine of the West Indies and place of retreat to the island of Barbados' was predictably unacceptable and, in any case, far too expensive. He was followed by another engineer, Christian Lilly (who was also responsible for drawing up the original plans for Codrington College, on the eastern side of the island), who reported in 1705 that he found the island to be 'altogether in a very weak and defenceless condition ... the western part of the island is almost everywhere open for an enemy to land, and there is no such thing in the country as deserves the name of a fort'. He prepared an elaborate plan to strengthen Charles Fort by the addition of a 'little castle or detached bastion' to be named St. Ann's (always spelt without an 'e') in honour of the reigning monarch, Queen Anne.

The fort was eventually constructed as a separate unit on high ground about 700 yards to the east of Charles Fort and by 1713 consisted of a hexagon of massive walls enclosing an area of about an acre and a half that is essentially all that there is today (53). It was calculated that it would contain at least 300 men but, cooped up as they would have been without water, a bombproof magazine, or protection against bombardment and the elements, they could not have held out for long.

Like all the island's early forts and batteries, both Charles Fort and St. Ann's Fort came under the authority of the Commissioners of the Fortifications and were manned by the Barbados Militia. They were not taken over by the British Army and integrated into the Garrison until 1836 and 1811 respectively.

The Establishment of the Garrison (1780–1801)

The declaration of war on Britain, on 28 June 1778, by France, in alliance with the newly independent United States of America, and the despatch of orders that same day by Louis XVI to the Governor-General of Martinique, the Marquis de Bouillé, directing him to 'attack and take' Britain's possessions in the West Indies, resulted in an entirely new military situation which did not, however, at first seem to warrant the construction of permanent garrison buildings as such.

The orders reached Martinique on 15 August and, on the morning of 7 September, French forces invaded and captured the neighbouring island of Dominica, to be followed the next year in June by the taking of St. Vincent, and in July of Grenada. There could be no doubt that the French intended, before long, to attempt the seizure of Barbados. Therefore the British Government decided to send regular troops to Barbados under the command of Major-General Sir John Vaughan, with Admiral Sir George Rodney in command of the naval forces in the West Indies.

The Barbados Government was not aware of these intentions until General Vaughan actually arrived in mid-February 1780 with the 89th Regiment; the President of the Council, John Dotin, then acting as Governor, found himself hurriedly having to find accommodation for this totally unexpected influx of troops. A number of buildings located in what are now Bridge and Marhill Streets in Bridgetown were requisitioned to house the officers and men, while a house was found for General Vaughan on Constitution Hill in the grounds of the present Queen's Park. In October that same year Barbados was devastated by a violent hurricane and the troops that arrived the following year had to be billeted in such forts and batteries as had been repaired.

In October 1782 President Dotin found himself obliged to notify the Secretary of State that, on account of the island's impoverished state, it had become impossible for him to find accommodation for the additional troops which were due to arrive. Instructions were then sent to Major-General Gabriel Christie, by then commanding the forces, to erect temporary barracks. The following December the General bought the property he occupied on Constitution Hill, consisting of 14 acres, and in 1783 he had a barracks some 300 feet long constructed on the west side of his house. The house itself, which had been damaged by the hurricane during General Vaughan's occupancy, was then demolished by General Christie and a new one intended for himself and his successors completed by the end of 1783; this was known as King's House, until in Queen Victoria's reign the name was changed to Queen's House, the name it still bears today.

After the American War of Independence ended in 1783, and the French threat was apparently removed, the British troops were withdrawn from Barbados, leaving only a small token force. Realizing, apparently rather belatedly, the seriousness of the task of re-establishing law and order and providing protection from possible future attacks, particularly on the islands recently returned to Britain by the Treaty of Versailles—St. Kitts, Nevis, Montserrat, Grenada, the Grenadines, St. Vincent and Dominica—the British Government decided, in 1785, to establish land forces permanently in the Windward and Leeward Islands, with Barbados as their headquarters. Two military engineers, Colonel Henry Gordon and Lieutenant Robert D'Arcy, were sent to prepare plans for a Garrison in Barbados and, after making a survey of the entire area south-east of Bridgetown, they at first thought that the Graeme Hall district of Christ Church was best suited for the construction of garrison buildings. Finally, however, they decided on the area near Charles Fort and St. Ann's Castle, and began making plans for its fortification. Thus the establishment of a permanent Garrison began.

In September 1788 Lieutenant Colonel Andrew Frazer, commanding the Royal Engineers in the West Indies, submitted proposals to the Governor, David Parry, for the purchase of about 60 acres of land, most of which lay approximately between Charles Fort and St. Ann's Castle, and in February 1789 the Army bought its first lot, consisting of 16 acres. This was the area extending eastward from what is now the Barbados Light and Power Company headquarters and included roughly one third of the area of the Savannah, with the Bush Hill district. By the end of 1790 additional purchases of land along the coast had increased the garrison site to 64 acres.

St. Ann's Castle, or Fort, with its 14 and a half acres, was not included in these transactions since, like Charles Fort, it belonged to the Government of the Colony of Barbados, and not to the Imperial Government. However, when construction of the garrison buildings was started in 1789, the British Army was allowed to build its Powder Magazine and Ordnance Storehouse in the grounds of the Castle and the large barracks known at one time as the Drill Hall (55) over the ditch on the north face of the Castle itself.

By 1793 there were in addition the two barrack buildings originally both called the Stone Barracks (47/48) and by 1801 another barracks some 300 ft long by 50 ft wide had been erected approximately where the Iron Barracks (49) now stands; this was a wooden building still in existence in 1818 but demolished sometime before 1822; the Iron Barracks was erected in its place in 1842. The barrack square lay between these three buildings. Another major garrison building erected between 1793 and 1801 was the Commissariat Provision Store (73). Meanwhile, the barracks on Constitution Hill, erected in 1783, still stood. It continued to be occupied as late as 1818 but, like the other wooden buildings at St. Ann's, it had been demolished by 1822.

During the last few years of the eighteenth century, which included the French Revolution in 1789 and subsequent war with Revolutionary France, the Caribbean became a major theatre of operations, in which Barbados was the centre of the stage. She provided the launching pad for attacks on neighbouring territories in enemy hands, and all troops in the island were either about to form part of such expeditions or were available as reinforcements for the defence of other British colonies, if these were threatened with invasion. The Garrison, however, in spite of the attention paid to it, evidently provided totally inadequate housing for the officers and men who were continually passing through; troops were frequently accommodated, sometimes under canvas, in the Brittons Hill and Dayrells Road areas, or even as far afield as Oistins, Speightstown and elsewhere. A private in the Royal Scots Fusiliers, for example, writing home to report his arrival, said that some of the troops were under canvas 'at a part of the island which, being mountainous, is named Scotland'. Clearly, the time was ripe for some expansion of the existing garrison buildings.

The Expansion of the Garrison (1802–1815)

The renewed outbreak of war with France in 1803 led to the rapid expansion of the Barbados Garrison as a headquarters for Britain's land forces in the Windward and Leeward Islands and necessitated the acquisition of more land and the construction of additional buildings to house the officers and men. Indeed, the year 1802 marked the beginning of the expansion of St. Ann's Garrison beyond what had hitherto been called the 'King's Boundary'. During that year and the next a total of about 48 acres of land was purchased extending eastward into the lower Dayrells Road area, taking in the ground where the three brick barracks were later erected (18/28/29); around the same time a parcel of eight and a half acres to the east of the Garrison area was acquired as a site for a new General Hospital, built between 1803 and 1806.

Construction on the west side of the Savannah–the Parade Ground–had apparently started about 1790 with the building of

The Main Guard as seen from the Stone Barracks (Arthur Pigott, 1839)

an Ordnance Hospital and its ancillary buildings as well as what appear to have been two houses for the medical staff (5/6/7). These were all located at the top of Bush Hill, along with the present Bush Hill House (10), which was purchased as quarters for the Commanding Officer of the Royal Engineers. The Main Guard (1/2) was built in 1804 followed in 1812 by the adjacent barracks for the Royal Military Artificers, Sappers and Miners (3). The ground at the rear, and below these buildings, lying opposite what is now the Barbados Light and Power Company, was occupied initially by the Military Stables and the storehouses of the Quartermaster-General's Department then later by the workshops of the Royal Engineers (8).

Construction on the east side of the Savannah did not start until later. In 1805 Barbados was threatened with attack from French naval forces; the timely appearance, however, of a British fleet under the command of Admiral Nelson, and his victory at Trafalgar in October of that year, lifted the immediate threat of invasion, but the Governor, Lord Seaforth, informed the British Government of his concern for the island's security in the longer term. In response, materials were sent out for building additional barracks capable of housing 800 more troops and the request was made for the Colony to provide 'negro' labour to aid in constructing the buildings. The result was the three brick barracks east of the Savannah (18/28/29) which were built between August 1807 and the end of 1808.

Other land acquired in 1802 was the greater portion of the land of 'Shot Hall' (68) for the Engineers' Department. This extended almost to what is now the Bay Street Esplanade; at its northern boundary a long narrow pond running parallel to the seashore turned sharply eastward bisecting Bay Street. The Army was obliged to bridge this stream in order to facilitate communication with Bridgetown, and the Barrier Bridge (69/70/71), as it was called, remained until 1884, when the road to Hastings was being prepared for the lines of the newly established tramway.

Also acquired in 1802 was the ground lying between the Commissariat Provision Store and the road leading to Gravesend beach, and in 1804 the Commissariat Rum Store (67) was erected there, with a capacity of 500 casks; it was apparently built in preparation for the Royal Navy's Dockyard (62), which was to be established the following year. A small Guard Room, at that time

The Brick Barracks (Lieut. J.M. Carter, 1836)

of wood (63), probably housed the guard for the Rum Store. The existence of the Naval Dockyard necessitated the establishment of a Naval Hospital, and this was built, of wood, on 22 acres to the east of the Garrison. Opened in 1806 and closed in 1816, with the shutting down of the dockyard on the transfer of the naval headquarters to Antigua, both the remnants of the dockyard and the hospital were destroyed in the hurricane of 1831.

Further expansion took place within the St. Ann's District with the purchase in 1811 of six and a quarter acres of land from the property later called Dalkeith, and about 1817 the 'New Prison' was built on that site and enlarged in 1853 (17). In 1814 a property called 'The Banyans', situated at the junction of Bay Street and Chelsea Road, was acquired and became the residence of the Officer Commanding the Royal Artillery and in later years that of the Deputy Assistant Adjutant-General; of this nothing now remains with the exception of a remnant of the Garrison Wall (72), which,

along with other sections of the wall segregating military property from adjacent private property, was probably built prior to 1844.

During this period further buildings and land were acquired which lay outside the Garrison. These included the property called 'the Retreat', situated near King's House, which was bought in about 1804 as quarters for the Deputy Adjutant-General, and the 'Pavilion', erected at the rear of King's House for the Military Secretary. Among these was a site on Bay Street purchased in 1805 for the erection of an office for the Deputy Adjutant-General.

By this time the Garrison, and the buildings associated with it, had expanded to approximately its present size. From this time on, with the cessation of the wars with France, and with the ravages of the hurricane of 1831, it can only be considered to have entered into a period at least of change, or perhaps more accurately, of decline.

The Decline of the Garrison Including the Hurricane of 1831 (1816–1905)

With the end in 1815 of the wars with France the nature and functions of the Garrison changed materially. It was no longer a launching pad for offensive or defensive expeditions to other parts of the region but, continuing as it did as the headquarters of the Windward and Leeward Islands Command, it was the scene of a large number of troop movements both within the area and to and from other stations.

As the strength of the Garrison declined – it fell from about 2700 in 1815 to a figure fluctuating until 1854 at a little under 1500, and from 1858 onward consisted usually of one regiment supplemented by a detachment of a West India regiment – so the functions of certain of the buildings changed. One example is the building on Bay Street which was purchased in 1817 for the offices of the Deputy Adjutant-General and Deputy Quartermaster-General, later becoming the office of the Garrison Headquarters Staff and then, from 1883 to 1887, functioning as the United Services Home, a recreational centre for the Army and the Navy, and finally as Married Quarters for the Deputy Adjutant-General's Staff. Another is the Ordnance Barracks on the west side of the Savannah which toward the end of the century was used to house the instruments of the regimental band.

There were, however, now certain internal security problems to be dealt with. The slave insurrection which broke out in April 1816 in the parish of St. Philip, and was put down within a couple of days with the assistance of a British regiment from the Garrison, caused the white population of the island to call for precautions to be taken against anything of the sort happening again. As a

Looking toward the area of the Naval Dockyard (1852)

result, a chain of signal stations, manned by Royal Artillery personnel, was established, of which Gun Hill, in St. George, and Moncrieffe, in St. Philip, were used by the Army as places for rest and recuperation. Gun Hill, in particular, which was transferred to the Army in 1818 and had 20 acres attached to it, was used from 1842 as a refuge when there were epidemics of yellow fever in the Garrison.

An important feature of the earlier part of this period was undoubtedly the hurricane of 1831, which is referred to as an 'awful visitation' on the monument now standing at the top of Bush Hill (9). It speedily reduced the island to almost total ruin and caused more than 2000 casualties, most of them fatal. The Garrison area was obviously very severely damaged. The Governor's despatch, dated the day after the hurricane, reported that 'the barracks and hospitals of St. Ann's are in a state of complete dilapidation and ruin, and I have been under the necessity of ordering troops under canvas'. Another account said that 'almost every building on the Garrison was demolished' and another that 'had the area suffered a bombardment it could not have presented a more deplorable appearance than it did after the storm'. One particularly poignant sight must have been that of the Officers' New Building (29) which was in the process of being decorated for a Grand Ball scheduled to take place the evening after the hurricane struck.

Among the installations which were virtually annihilated were the Naval Dockyard (62), where 'the desolation was awful and lamentable in the extreme', the Garrison market place, which was built on pillars and of which nothing remained, and the Military General Hospital and Naval Hospital; of these only the Military Hospital was later to be rebuilt. Almost every other building suffered some damage, with the exception, it appears, of the new

Ordnance Hospital (32/33/34) which was stated by one observer to be the only building of large dimensions that escaped injury due to the fact that its framework was of iron.

The units then occupying the Garrison were detachments of the Royal Artillery, the Royal Sappers and Miners, the 35th, 36th Regiments and a detachment of the 1st West India Regiment. In addition there were the Corps of Military Labourers, the Infirmary Establishment, and the Commissariat staff. They all suffered casualties, amounting to 48 killed and 294 injured, 52 of these seriously. The dead of the 35th Regiment were interred in the Military Cemetery (57) at Gravesend and the other victims in large pits dug in the slope opposite the ruins of the Military General Hospital at Hastings, where the 'awful visitation' monument was originally located.

Repair work started almost immediately. Four days after the event the Officer of Ordnance was taking on extra labourers, including 'twelve extra Negro labourers', and 'six white labourers at 1s. 11d. per diem and sixteen black labourers at 1s. 8¾d. per diem'. By November that same year such Garrison buildings as had merely been damaged had been repaired, while those that had been demolished, with several exceptions, were rebuilt apparently within a couple of years.

Important lessons concerning the construction of buildings were no doubt learned from this most destructive of hurricanes although the matter had already been under consideration for some time, and the desirability of using iron girders and joists recommended. Captain Brandreth, R.E., who reported in 1844 on work he had carried out on the implementation of recommendations made in 1824 noted that 'it is of the utmost importance, when any building is designed, to consider the means of guarding against the hurricanes that constantly occur in the West Indies' and that 'to persons unacquainted with the tropics, it is hardly possible to convey a notion of the effects of a hurricane on buildings apparently of the strongest construction'. Interestingly enough, the one building in the Garrison which he cites as an example of satisfactory construction is the new Ordnance Hospital which 'sustained no material injury from the hurricane, whilst almost all the buildings in the neighbourhood were destroyed, or severely damaged'. This was evidently due to the use of iron in its construction. It may well have been as a result both of previous recommendations, and the experience of 1831, that extensive use was made of iron in the construction of the Iron Barracks (49) in 1842.

Although all the wooden buildings in the Garrison and elsewhere were destroyed, never to be rebuilt, the stone buildings were for the most part able to be repaired, and no lasting scars seem to have been left.

Life in the Garrison, particularly in the latter part of this period, must have been considerably more peaceful than it had been in its heyday, even though there were still occasional internal security matters to be dealt with, such as the Confederation Riots of 1876, during which the Police were assisted by elements of the 2nd West India Regiment and the 35th Regiment, when two rioters were killed and five died from wounds. It was then that, tedious as life may still have appeared to some, serious attempts were made to improve conditions for both officers and men. A picture begins to emerge of some aspects of life, and death, in the Garrison and of its transformation, toward the end of the century, into an area of some charm and social dalliance, where the ladies of Barbados would gather in the late afternoons, to listen to the regimental band, and gossip with, and no doubt about, their friends and acquaintances.

Life and Death in St. Ann's Garrison

Life was both uncomfortable and boring, and death was everywhere, as Captain H.W. Bunbury of the 33rd Regiment notes in his letters, written from Barbados in 1841 and 1842. He relates how, at that time, there were nearly 2500 troops stationed in the Garrison, though this is likely to have been an over-estimate, and that barrack accommodation existed for only 1000 at the most. The greater number had to occupy tents, and one regiment had to sleep on the bare ground, without even blankets to cover them—these would have been essential for protection against insects and vermin even if not against the cold. Though quarters for officers were rather more adequate than for the men they were by no means comfortable; Captain Bunbury recounts that, although each officer had one room to himself, divided into two sections by a low partition, and that the rooms were 'well enough', they were disgracefully dirty, out of repair, and swarming with all kinds of vermin.

Boredom also prevailed, according to Bunbury. Outside the daily

*View of Carlisle Bay and Bridgetown from the Stone Barracks
(Arthur Pigott, 1839)*

routine of parades and drill, conducted in the early morning and
late afternoon, there was little to do, and the sole occupation of
most of the officers consisted of lounging about on the galleries
and smoking cigars. There was, it appears, a small library, with
a billiard room attached, but the subscription to the former was
exorbitant. As for the rank and file, it is not clear what welfare
facilities were available, but it seems that, outside their working
hours, they were left very much to their own devices. These,
predictably, included the excessive consumption of rum, which on
occasions resulted in the commission of serious crimes. One private
soldier on being sentenced to death for the attempted murder of
his commander made a short speech warning his comrades against
drunkenness even as the firing party moved into position, but
official attempts to ban the sale of liquor to non-commissioned
personnel proved unsuccessful. It seems that it was not until 1854
that any serious attempt was made to provide educational and

other facilities for other ranks, when the former Ordnance Hospital (32/33/34) was converted into a soldiers' library and recreation room.

In addition, there were few facilities, during the early part of the century, for the observance of religion. An independent observer, writing in 1825, reports that such religious services as there were consisted merely of the chaplain's reading a few prayers on the open parade ground, a proceeding that was 'really a complete farce, and so understood to be'. The attitude of the British Government appears to have been no better; when Governor Sir Lionel Smith wrote to the Secretary of State for the Colonies in August 1833 concerning the 'expediency' of erecting a Garrison church, the response came back that he would 'not be justified in applying to Parliament to provide the funds necessary'.

Some time later the situation improved with services for the soldiers being held in a barrack room and then, in 1848, when St. Matthias church was officially opened, the British Government agreed to pay £75 a year to enable the troops to worship there. On Sundays the Anglican chaplain conducted a service at 8 a.m. for those off duty, while the incumbent conducted another at 4.30 p.m. for those who could not attend in the morning. These arrangements evidently continued until a Garrison chapel was finally erected, in about 1855, on the site north-east of the Savannah where the house called 'Little Heath' now stands (36/37). This building was demolished sometime after 1905 when it passed into private hands but it seems that no record of it remains except occasional references to an altar rail, now in St. Lawrence church, and a hymn book used by the organist.

Soldiers of the Roman Catholic persuasion had no chaplain until 1839, when a priest took up residence in the island and was appointed chaplain to the Garrison. He seems to have held services in a room until St. Patrick's Roman Catholic church was built in 1848, which was attended on Sundays by Roman Catholic soldiers. After the building was destroyed by fire in 1897, the chaplain continued to hold services in the Garrison schoolroom, until the new church was built in 1899. In recognition of St. Patrick's status as a Garrison church the badges of several regiments were placed on its walls in 1903, and can still be seen there.

Perhaps the worst aspect of life in the Garrison, for the greater part of its occupation by British troops, was the prevalence of

Cenotaph in the Military Cemetery

diseases of various sorts. As Bunbury says: 'this is certainly a melancholy part of the world to live in; the constant scene of sickness and death'. During the earlier years particularly, the Savannah became a swamp during the rainy season, and this and the crab holes that abounded, especially in the coastal areas, provided prolific breeding places for the mosquitoes which no one knew at the time were the carriers of yellow fever. In 1811 alone, yellow fever carried off 249 men in the Garrison out of a total strength of 2040 (some 12 per cent) and by the end of 1823 an aggregate of 1619 men had died of the disease; most of them were buried in the low-lying area to the south-west of St. Ann's Fort where, it is said, the coffins were simply allowed to sink into the bog. Not long after assuming command in 1817 of the Army in the Windward and Leeward Islands (and the Governorship of Barbados) Lieutenant-General Viscount Combermere had a drainage system laid down beneath the Savannah—it still exists—and this proved helpful. But the mortality rate continued to be relatively high; during 1849, for example, the year of a particularly violent epidemic of yellow fever, the number of deaths was nearly 128 per 1000.

Beginning in 1842 it became customary, on an outbreak of an epidemic of yellow fever, to transfer the British troops to the healthier air of Gun Hill in St George or sometimes to Brittons' Hill. However, in 1881, after an outbreak had claimed a number of lives, the troops were temporarily withdrawn from the island altogether and sent off to England.

Next to yellow fever, the commonest causes of mortality among the Garrison troops were abdominal diseases such as dysentery and diarrhoea. The incidence of these, however, began declining from the 1850s with the application of stricter measures to protect the sources of drinking water against contamination. Nevertheless, the overcrowding already noted by Captain Bunbury cannot have helped to improve the situation nor can the level of hygiene; a report of the mid nineteenth century refers, for example, to the fact that it was compulsory for the troops to wash their feet twice a week.

A further problem was that of venereal diseases and in 1869, on the recommendation of the British Government, which had recently enacted legislation to safeguard its armed forces in this respect, the Barbados Government opened a Contagious Diseases Hospital, partly built and maintained with grants from the Imperial Government. Popularly known as 'The Lock', this hospital (situated in what later became the Harbour Police compound on Bay Street) operated under the provisions of a local Contagious Diseases Act (1868) which required all known or suspected prostitutes to be registered, given compulsory medical examinations and treated if necessary. The Act operated effectively for some years but later less so; records show that during the last quarter of 1882, at any rate, no less than 105 of the troops in the Garrison were under treatment for venereal diseases. With the repeal of the Imperial Contagious Diseases Act in 1886, and the consequent withdrawal of the British Government's subsidy, the local Act was also repealed (in 1887) and the Lock Hospital closed.

In spite of all its negative aspects, Garrison life could still be enjoyed at least to a certain extent, as Bunbury himself indicates when he exhorts friends in England not to be uneasy on his account

Race Day on the Savannah (W.S. Hedges, 1846)

for 'we act plays, dance or dine out just as we should in any place where no such fatal disease prevails'. Indeed, the extent of his correspondence must have done much to keep the boredom away, as no doubt did the drawing and painting carried out by Ensigns A. Piggott and C.M. Wilson in the late 1830s, quite apart from passing on to later generations such invaluable records of the Garrison and its life. In addition, there were efforts made at an official level to do something to improve what would nowadays be called the 'quality of life' from quite early in the nineteenth century.

One such effort was the founding in 1805 of the St. Ann's Cricket Club by a group of officers and, it appears, some civilians who were connected with the Garrison; thus cricket was introduced into Barbados.

Another was the promotion of amateur dramatics attributed to Lord Combermere, soon after he took office in 1817. The first public performance took place in July 1818 in a wooden building on the east side of St. Ann's Fort, formerly used as a barracks and later as a hospital. This was replaced in 1823 with a specially constructed

The Savannah (1853)

wooden building roughly opposite the Seaview Hotel, which was in turn replaced by a new Garrison Theatre in 1842 – Bunbury was to be its stage manager and writes of it with satisfaction – and when this was demolished in 1868, theatrical activity shifted to the Garrison Recreation room to the east of the Savannah (probably 33). The theatre moved in 1893 to what had been the Commissariat Provision Store (73).

One other activity that became established in the Garrison was racing. Held originally at the appropriately named Newmarket in St. George and then later at Wildey in St. Michael, this was shifted to the Savannah in about 1846 with the permission of the military authorities, who no doubt saw this as a useful form of recreational activity for both officers and men.

Indeed, it was during the middle of the century, and particularly after the drop in the average strength of the Garrison from 1854 onward (the number of men fell to about 1000), that living conditions generally started to improve. One account of Barbados published in 1886 tells of cricket matches, athletics and a variety of sporting activities taking place on the Parade Ground (the

Savannah). Another describes 'a military band discoursing sweet music' on such occasions, of officers and men dispensing hospitality to their friends under the shade of marquees and tents, and says that these meetings were a sight worth seeing, what with the 'fluttering pennons, the picturesque uniforms of the Zouave soldiers of the West India regiments; the red or white of the British infantry'.

The Dissolution of the British Military Garrison (1905–1906)

During the last years of the century the British Government had been contemplating the removal of the forces from the West Indies and, in 1894, the Secretary of State for the Colonies, the Earl of Ripon, addressed a circular despatch to the various colonial governments containing proposals for the disposal of colonial military property when no longer required by the forces.

Several years were, however, to pass before any further action was taken but, finally, at the beginning of January 1905 the Governor of Barbados, Sir Gilbert Carter, was notified by telegram (communications were now being speeded up) from the Secretary of State that the British Government intended to withdraw the troops from the island at an early date. In future, security for the West Indian colonies would be provided by a fast naval cruiser permanently stationed in the region, while a naval squadron would visit every winter.

The island's legislature was dismayed when informed of the impending removal of the troops, partly no doubt out of the loss to the local economy of some £80 000 a year which was then a considerable sum of money. The House of Assembly drew up a petition to the Sovereign, King Edward VII, expressing regret at his Government's decision and asking for the matter to be reconsidered. The Governor was, however, obliged to affirm that the decision of the British Government was irrevocable.

Thus, in November 1905, the last British troops remaining in the Garrison sailed away from Barbados, followed in January 1906 by a battalion of the 1st West India Regiment. Only a few staff officers and NCOs remained to wind up departmental affairs

The Savannah today (aerial view)

relating to the British Military Garrison, which had ceased to exist after 126 years.

In disposing of the various military installations those which properly belonged to the Barbados Government–Charles Fort, St. Ann's Fort, and Gun Hill signal station–were handed back; among these was the barracks on the north face of St. Ann's Fort, which was fitted up in 1909 as a drill hall and gymnasium for the Barbados Volunteer Force (formed in 1902), with three rooms on the ground floor allocated to the Police Force for use as a guard house. Of the other buildings and installations which were the responsibility of the British War Department, the Barbados Government bought Queen's House and its associated buildings, including the Deputy Adjutant-General's Building on Bay Street and, after leasing the Savannah, bought it outright in 1912, with the proviso that it be kept as an open space and available for military exercises 'in the event of the military reoccupation of the island'; in the same year it also bought the Military Prison, the three neighbouring barrack blocks and the Married Women's Quarters; the last of these was demolished in 1974 to make way for the Garrison Secondary School. Of the buildings within the St. Ann's Fort complex the three barrack blocks—the Iron Barracks and the two Stone Barracks (one of which was commonly called the West India Barracks)—were War Department property and, after being leased by private persons, were bought by the Government in 1929.

Of the other installations there are several of which little remains, as for example the Naval Dockyard, reduced to a single building within the Mobil Oil compound, the Naval Hospital, the site of which is now a residential area called Navy Gardens, and the Garrison Chapel, of which there is virtually no trace remaining. There are, however, a number of buildings which are in private hands, including the former Medical Pavilion (now unhappily nothing but a shell) and the Military Hospital, acquired in 1928 and converted into residential apartments known collectively as Pavilion Court, and several smaller ones, now private residences. One building, without doubt the best known in the Garrison, is the Main Guard, purchased privately in 1906 and turned into the Savannah Club, which was acquired by Government at the beginning of 1989 and is to revert to its original title of Main Guard; it was used by Government as a back-drop to the celebrations on the Savannah marking the 21st anniversary of Independence and its planned restoration and adaptive use will enable it to reclaim something of its former dignity.

TOURS OF THE GARRISON
HISTORIC AREA

Suggested tours of the three main segments of the Garrison Historic Area follow. Each tour is shown on a separate map; the buildings which formed part of the original Garrison are outlined in red, with the names by which they are generally known today given in brackets for ease when requesting directions from passers-by. Those which are not Garrison buildings are outlined in black and are included as points of reference, with descriptions only in the case of buildings of particular interest. Information is also included on a number of buildings outside the Garrison Historic Area.

TOUR 'A': AREA IMMEDIATELY SURROUNDING THE SAVANNAH

These buildings, surrounding what was previously the main parade ground, are generally regarded as comprising the most important section of the Garrison Historic Area, though they are not the oldest. In fact, the buildings themselves date back in the main to the expansion of the Garrison in the first part of the nineteenth century; the Parade Ground for most of that century was the scene of many ceremonial events and sporting activities—a tradition which continues today, with the use of the Savannah for Independence Parades and for organized sports, such as cricket, football and racing, and less formal activities, such as walking, jogging, 'liming', or simply 'cooling out'.

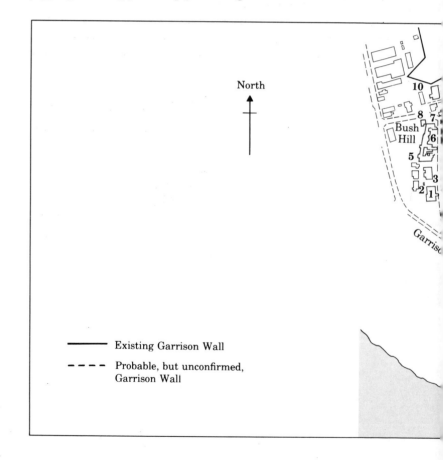

North

———— Existing Garrison Wall

– – – – Probable, but unconfirmed, Garrison Wall

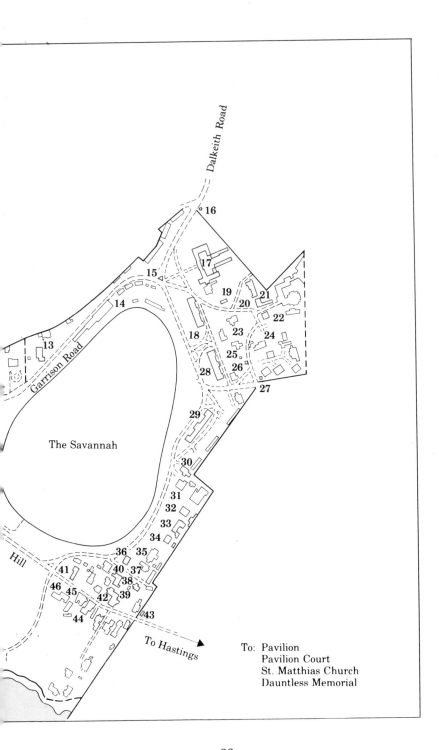

Dalkeith Road

16

17

15

19

21

14

20

22

18

23

24

13

Garrison Road

25

26

28

27

The Savannah

29

30

31

32

33

34

Hill

36 35

41

40 37

38

46 45

42 39

44

43

To Hastings

To: Pavilion
     Pavilion Court
     St. Matthias Church
     Dauntless Memorial

The Main Guard (1871)

1/2 *The Main Guard* (Savannah Club)

This central point of the Garrison, looking out over what was originally the Parade Ground, was built in 1804. It was used for, among other things, courts martial, with the prisoners being housed in the small guard house to the north. One interesting feature is the clock, which bears the date 1803, and was made by Dwerri and Carter of London, a noted clockmaker; it is possible that two of the dials were added at a later date. Another is the coat of arms, which seems likely to have been added between 1816 and 1837 and may have been made of 'coadestone', an artificial stone made of clay and fired in a kiln and used at that period for a number of monuments, including the lion on the south side of Westminster Bridge in London.

The verandah and portico, with their cast-iron trimmings, were added after the purchase of the building in 1906 by Mr. Darnley Da Costa, Senior, and its conversion to use as a private club, until 1989, when it was acquired by Government.

Coat of arms on the pediment of the Main Guard

The Main Guard with the small guard house

3 _Ordnance, or Royal Artillery, Barracks_ (Stafford House)

Built in 1812, but by the end of the century, when gunners were no longer required, it was used to house the military band and its instruments.

After its sale in 1906 it was at first a private house, then became a guest house, and was later converted into apartments; the present external finish (which has caused some visitors to mistake it for a modern building) conceals interesting brick and stone work.

4 _The Cannon_

There were previously nine cannon displayed here, which were removed in 1966 to grace the remnants of Charles Fort at the newly constructed Hilton Hotel. These were returned in 1988, and form the nucleus of the present National Cannon Collection. Details of the Collection, including one cannon which dates back to Oliver Cromwell's time, follow p 67.

5/6/7 _Officers' Quarters_ (Horseshoe Manor, The Bungalow and Caledon)

There were quarters here for officers of the Royal Artillery and Royal Engineers by 1824 but changes over the years, and particularly since their purchase by private individuals after 1905, make it impossible to identify the original buildings precisely.

On the site across the road, where there were until recently tennis courts and which is now an extension of the race course, there was by 1804 an Ordnance Hospital, built in stone, with outbuildings in wood; this was condemned in 1822, as being in too confined a position, and keeping the breeze away from the officers' quarters opposite, and by 1828 it was no longer in existence. A new hospital was built on the opposite side of the Savannah (32/33/34).

The 'lantern'

8 *Regimental Engineers' Quarters* (Coniston)

This house, described as above on a plan of 1843, is all that remains of the Engineers' Yard, which once extended down to Bay Street; steps at the back led up to the Royal Engineers' Officers' Quarters (5/6/7) but the entrance was bricked up in 1844. An interesting architectural feature is the 'lantern', which may not only have allowed for the escape of hot air but also provided a look-out for the engineer in residence.

At the time of the sale of the house in 1905 it was the residence of the Clerk of Works.

9 *Monument*

This monument, of a design frequently seen in British garrisons abroad, commemorates 'the fourteen soldiers and one married woman who were killed by the destruction of the Barracks and Hospital during the awful visitation of the hurricane 11 August 1831'.

It was originally located opposite the Military Hospital but moved here in 1906.

Water mill and bath house at the entrance to Bush Hill House

10/11 *Commanding Officer Royal Engineers' Quarters* (Bush Hill House)

The original house on this site has been identified as the one where George Washington stayed when he visited Barbados in 1751 (rather than the one on Bay Street now known as George Washington House although there were no houses in the area at that date). The present house was in existence in 1804 and is the oldest residence in the Garrison Historic Area. In 1824 it was described as built of stone, on two floors, and measuring 55 ft by 50 ft. It has suffered many changes over the years.

The water mill and bath house situated just inside the compound were already in existence by 1793.

12 *Royal Bank of Canada House*

This Canadian style house dates back to the 1920s and has been modified for use by the Bank as offices.

13 *Sergeants' Married Quarters* (Defence Force Married Quarters)

Date back the mid nineteenth century but have undergone many changes.

14 *Barbados Turf Club Stands*

15 *Monument*

Commemorates those who fell in action in Martinique and Guadeloupe in 1809 and 1810. It originally stood in the grounds of St. Ann's Fort, near the south corner of the Stone Barracks (48); it was damaged in the 1831 hurricane but restored in 1838 and transferred to its present site in 1906.

Monument opposite the Museum

16 *Gateposts*

Of these gate posts the one numbered WD 24 is probably in its original position at the North Gate of the Garrison; the other, at the corner of Chelsea Road (the number WD 23 is now located a little way down the road), was moved into this position with widening of the road in 1885.

17 *Military Prison* (Barbados Museum)

The 'New Prison', built in 1817–1818, is the area which is now known as the Upper Courtyard; the rest of the buildings, completed in 1853, surround what was formerly a concrete exercise ground. The complex was leased by the Government to the newly formed Barbados Museum and Historical Society in 1933 and in recent years has undergone considerable modification, including the grassing over of the exercise yard, without upsetting the integrity of the buildings and their surroundings. A new wing, to the south of the original buildings, was opened in 1989.

Southern side of the Upper Courtyard of the Museum

Block 'A' seen from the Savannah

18 *Barracks* (Block 'A', housing Caribbean Examinations Council)

Built in 1807–1808 this building, together with Block 'B' (28), was referred to in 1824 as the 'New Barracks', when they were both described as being of brick, on two floors, housing 400 men each. They were severely damaged in the hurricane of 1831, but rebuilt. After being sold to Government in 1912 they were first used for residential purposes but later converted into offices.

19 *Latrine*

This probably served the nearby Barracks (now Block 'A').

20 *Married Men's Quarters* (Residence)

Described as such in 1822 when built of wood; many changes have taken place.

21 *Building With Turret* (Residence)

The eastern section of the building, with the turret, has a drainpipe with the date 1866 and contains seven cells, immediately adjoining the turret. It is believed that the turret was used to house officers requiring to be kept under restraint and it is possible that the whole building was an adjunct of the main prison, used for officers. At a later stage the building was converted for use as an infants' school.

22 *Married Non-Commissioned Officers' Quarters*

This was described as such in 1822 when it was built of wood; a stone building, erected after 1860, was known as the 'Singles' Mess'; it was renovated in 1934 and is now used by Government.

23 *Cookhouse*

This octagonal building is now used as a store.

24 *Venture*

A private residence built in the early 1920s.

25/26 *Latrine and Ablutions Buildings*

The larger building was used for ablutions, and the smaller as a latrine; it is hoped to restore both for use as a restaurant and toilet facilities.

Former latrine and ablutions buildings

27 *Gatepost*

This formed part of Schmidt's Gate, one of the four original entrances to the Garrison.

Gatepost forming part of Schmidt's Gate

28 *Barracks* (Block 'B', housing the Town and Country Planning Department Office)

See 18.

29 *Officers' Barrack* (Block 'C', housing several Government Offices)

Built in 1807–1808 at the same time as the other two barrack blocks, it was described in 1824 as built of brick, on two floors, measuring 250 ft by 50 ft. It was to be the scene of a Grand Ball on 12 August 1831 for which preparations were being made when the hurricane struck on the night of 10–11 August. After its sale to Government in 1912 it was used first for residential accommodation and later for offices.

30 *Stables* (Cherry Tree Cottage, now Offices for the Coast Guard)

In 1936 these stables were converted into a house by jacking up the·roof and inserting a second storey of sawn coral stone.

Building of the second storey of Cherry Tree Cottage (1936)

31 *Siesta*

A private residence built after the withdrawal of British forces.

32/33/34 *Ordnance Hospital* (Rafeen, Geneva, Letchworth—all private residences)

The construction of an Ordnance Hospital on this site was approved in 1826 as a replacement for the one on the other side of the Savannah (5/6/7). The iron work was sent out from England in 1828 and the building completed before the 1831 hurricane, during which it escaped serious damage due to the beams, joists and rafters being of iron. Of the three buildings the one known as Geneva was probably the main hospital; the ground floor was a hurricane shelter and the wards on the first floor, with verandahs all around them, were supported by iron pillars. In the 1860s (the Ordnance Department had been abolished in 1855 hence the need for a separate hospital) the building was converted for use as the soldiers'

'Geneva'—private residence

library and recreation room and also, it appears, utilised for amateur theatricals. Extensive alterations were made after the building passed into private hands, including a change in the level of the two storeys and the removal of the iron pillars to support the new ground floor verandah.

35 *Savannah Lodge* (Offices of, inter alia, the Caribbean Conservation Association)

Originally a store, this building was converted into a private residence known as Boylston and in 1927 was bought by Government as a residence for the Colonial Secretary and renamed Savannah Lodge; here lived, in the 1960s, Stewart Perowne and his wife Freya Stark.

36 *Site of Garrison Chapel* (part of the grounds of the residence Little Heath)

Tenders for the construction of the chapel had been requested in 1854 and plans show that it was already in existence in 1869 (St. Matthias church in Hastings had been used as the Garrison church since its consecration in 1850). The chapel, which had also been used as a school was sold in 1905 and demolished the following year.

37 *Little Heath*

Private residence (see 36 above).

38 *The Bower*

Private residence. It is believed that this was formerly a mortuary and was converted into a house when it was sold off in 1905; to date no confirmation of this has been found.

39 *Residence*

40 *Lucerne*

Private residence. Possibly former married soldiers' quarters.

41 *Brigade Major's Quarters* (Brigade House)

The single storey section is the earliest part of the building and was described in 1819 as the Brigade Major's Quarters; sometime after 1862 it became the residence of the chaplain, presumably because it was conveniently near the Garrison chapel, and remained as such until it was sold in 1905. The small square building to the east of the house was probably a dry pit latrine, with the slit windows so arranged that the air could enter but the occupants remain unseen. The two storey section was constructed after the building had passed into private hands.

The premises have been used as a home for elderly people and as an hotel and restaurant, but have recently been refurbished as doctors' consulting rooms.

The Brigade Major's Quarters

42 Site of Commandant's Quarters and Other Buildings (approximately area now occupied by the residence Hy Brasil)

The Commandant's Quarters were described in 1824 as being built of stone, on three floors, and measuring 59 ft by 32 ft but no trace remains of this apparently substantial building. Other buildings in much the same area were a specially constructed theatre put up in 1823, then replaced by a new Garrison theatre in 1842, which was demolished in 1868, after which theatricals took place in the Garrison Recreation Room (probably 33) until the move to the Commissariat Issuing Store (73) in 1893. Toward the end of the nineteenth century a racquets court and bowling alley were constructed on this site.

43 Garrison Wall

Part of the wall enclosing the south side of the Garrison; the South Gate was probably located here.

44 Seaview Hotel

This was not a Garrison building but is of interest as being of the same type of construction as the Charleston 'single house' (Barbados had close links with South Carolina from the latter's settlement until the mid eighteenth century) although it was probably built late in that century.

45 Parade View (Virginia Restaurant)

Not a Garrison building but an interesting example of a Palladian style suburban building, dating back to the early nineteenth century. After many years' disuse it was restored in 1987 for use as a restaurant.

46 Hastings Police Station

TOUR 'B': BUILDINGS WITHIN THE PERIMETER OF THE DEFENCE FORCE HEADQUARTERS

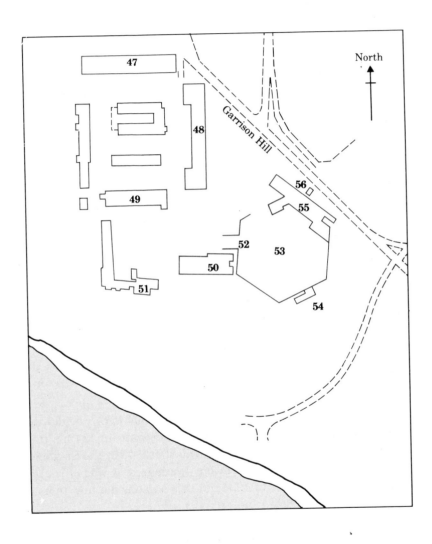

These buildings are the oldest in the Garrison, with the exception of Charles Fort. There is no public access to this area but guided tours can be arranged on application to the Chief of Staff of the Defence Force.

47 *Stone Barracks,* later *West India Barracks*

Completed by 1791, and originally known as the Stone Barracks, this building was described in 1824 as being of stone and brick, on two floors, measuring 265 ft by 44 ft and housing 450 men. It was badly damaged during the hurricane of 1831 and subsequently rebuilt. It became known as the West India Barracks when the West India Regiment had its mess and quarters there during the latter part of the nineteenth century. Between the departure of the British forces and the establishment of the Defence Force it provided living accommodation for government officials.

48 *Stone Barracks*

Also completed by 1791 and described in 1824 as officers' barracks it was damaged in the 1831 hurricane and rebuilt. After 1906 it was rented out as flats and in 1934 its name officially changed to St. Ann's Court. It has now reverted to its original name.

It should be noted that the cream colour of the recently restored buildings is the original colour of all Garrison buildings.

49 *Iron Barracks*

While there was a building on this site in 1804 it was evidently demolished and rebuilt, with an iron framework, in 1842; a full description of its construction was provided in 1843 by the Engineer in charge. After 1906 it was let out to tenants; it was officially renamed Queen's Court in 1934 but this name is not now in use.

50 *Magazine*

This magazine (and ordnance store) was built in 1789; it is still in use by the Defence Force.

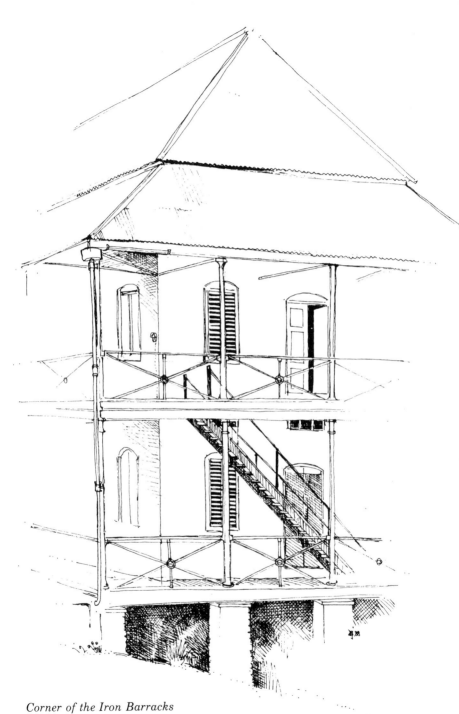

Corner of the Iron Barracks

51 *Residence of Ordnance Storekeeper* (now Defence Force Headquarters Offices)

Erected in 1811 as the residence, and probably also offices, of the Ordnance Storekeeper, it became the residence of the Adjutant when the Volunteer Force was formed shortly before the departure of the British Forces.

52 *Tunnel*

This leads from the present parade ground up to St. Ann's Fort and was constructed between 1817 and 1821.

53 *St. Ann's Fort*

Originally known as St. Ann's Castle, this consisted of a hexagon of massive walls, enclosing an area of an acre and a half, with a magazine in the centre; construction had started about 1705 but proceeded slowly owing to lack of funds. The magazine was demolished in 1811 as not being bomb-proof and its contents transferred to Charles Fort. A flagstaff was erected on this site, and later transferred to the top of the look-out tower constructed during the 1830s and which formed part of the island's signal system; it functioned during the 1914–1918 war as a wireless station in communication with ships as far away as the US coastal stations.

54 *Naval Magazine*

This magazine, which extends under St. Ann's Fort, probably dates back to the late eighteenth century. It is shown on the plan of 1822 as consisting of three bomb-proof casemates.

55 *Barracks/Armoury* (Drill Hall)

Built in 1790 as a soldiers' barracks it was designated in 1822 as an armoury to contain 12 000 stands of arms with offices for store-

keepers. From 1881 to 1905 it was the headquarters office for the Garrison; it reverted to the Government of Barbados in 1905 and was used as a gymnasium and drill hall for the Volunteer Force, at which time it was also available for rent by the public for dances, concerts and the like. It now houses the officers' and sergeants' messes of the Defence Force.

56 *Coastal Artillery Cannon*

At entrance of the Defence Force Officers' Mess.

TOUR 'C': FROM CHARLES FORT TO THE BARRIER BRIDGE

This tour includes Charles Fort, the oldest building in the Garrison, and extends through the area now dominated by the Hilton Hotel, Grand Barbados Beach Resort and the Mobil Oil Refinery, then along Bay Street to the Barrier Bridge entrance to the Garrison, located some hundred yards to the southeast of Government Headquarters.

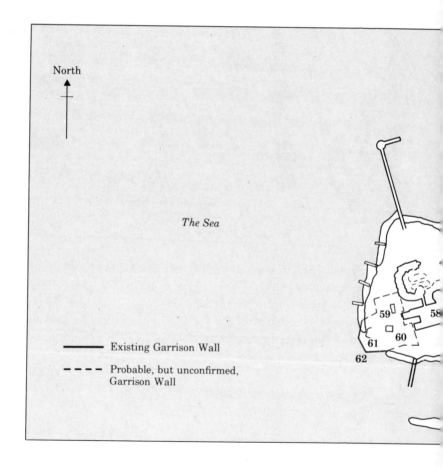

North

The Sea

——— Existing Garrison Wall

- - - - Probable, but unconfirmed, Garrison Wall

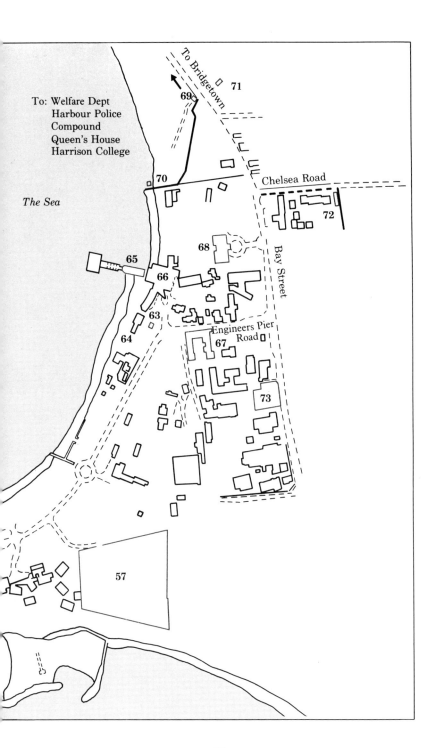

To Bridgetown

71

69

To: Welfare Dept
    Harbour Police
    Compound
    Queen's House
    Harrison College

70

The Sea

Chelsea Road

72

68

Bay Street

65

66

63

64

Engineers Pier
Road

67

73

57

The Barbados Military Cemetery with the Cross of Sacrifice

57 Barbados Military Cemetery

The area used as a burial ground was initially much larger but the present cemetery probably came into use about 1820, as that is the date of the first headstone. After the British troops left in 1905 the site deteriorated rapidly though in 1923 the Civic Circle undertook responsibility for its upkeep, including the construction of the wall, until it ran into financial difficulties. In 1975 the Barbados Military Cemetery Association was founded and the work started which resulted in the attractive and beautifully kept cemetery that it is today.

The Cross of Sacrifice was erected in 1982 and the Memorial Building at the entrance was completed in 1984 and contains information on the various military units involved in the Garrison and locations of the headstones. Past and present servicemen (and women) are eligible for burial here. To the right of the Cross of Sacrifice is a memorial to the former Prime Minister of Barbados, Errol Walton Barrow, who was a Flying Officer in the Royal Air Force.

58 Hilton Hotel

59/60/61 Charles Fort with Signal Station, Large Gun Emplacement and Cannon

Although the construction of the Hilton Hotel on this site has obscured much of Charles Fort, its original shape is easily visible from the air and from the sea. Originally called Needham's Fort but renamed Charles Fort at the restoration of Charles II in 1660, it was constructed in 1650 by the Barbados Militia and manned by its forces. It was not incorporated in the British Garrison until 1836, some fifty years after the decision had been taken to establish a garrison in the island. It was handed back to the Barbados Government on the withdrawal of British troops in 1905–1906.

The Needham's Point Signal Station, within the perimeter of the Fort, was erected about 1816 as one of the system of signal stations intended to provide early warning of a French attack, or of a slave

Charles Fort (aerial view)

uprising. Its original wooden superstructure was destroyed in the 1831 hurricane and replaced but again destroyed, this time by lightning, in 1929; a later one, of incorrect design, fell victim to termites. It is intended to replace the superstructure along the lines of the original one.

The large gun emplacement still has in position the tracks on which the gun moved; while the gun itself was reported to have been despatched to the United Kingdom during World War II to provide war material it was in fact too heavy and still remains in the vicinity and will eventually be replaced in its original position.

The cannon on the walls of the Fort are replicas of those that were moved here in 1966 from the Savannah but have since been put back there, and form part of the National Cannon Collection (see p.67).

62 *Cannon in the Sea and Naval Dockyard*

The recovery of these cannon is probably not practicable. En route from Charles Fort to the Small Guard Room (63) the area on the sea side, including part of the Mobil Oil Refinery, was formerly the site of the Naval Dockyard. This was built around 1805 but subsequently transferred to Antigua, the site of the naval head-quarters, and from about 1816 was used as a barracks. At the time of the 1831 hurricane it was described as 'Military Labourers' Barracks' and suffered serious damage. Little now remains of the Dockyard except for a building inside the Mobil Oil compound which has muskets as bars across the windows.

Ladies in mourning for King Edward VII receive a trophy in front of the small guard house (1910)

63 *Small Guard Room*

This building of wood in 1822, was later rebuilt in stone and probably housed the guard for the Rum Store (67). In 1904, just before the departure of the British Forces, the Barbados Rifle Association was founded and used the 'Hut', as it was called, as its club house. During World War II it was used by No. 1 Platoon of the Barbados Home Guard. In February 1987 its renovation was completed, through the efforts of the Garrison Committee and the Grand Barbados Beach Resort, and it is now used as an art gallery and boutique.

64 Barbados Cruising Club

65 Engineers' Pier (incorporated in the Grand Barbados Beach Resort)

This was already in existence in 1793; it was in regular use by the Army during the whole period of the existence of the Military Garrison. It formed part of a package, including Shot Hall (68), sold in 1906 to the Royal Mail Steam Packet Company. It was later used as a bathing station until its acquisition in 1928 by the Barbados Aquatic Club. It now forms part of the Grand Barbados Beach Resort.

66 Grand Barbados Beach Resort

67 Rum Store (Island Inn)

Built in 1804, it is shown in 1824 as the Commissariat Rum Store, built in stone, on one floor, measuring 250 ft by 31 ft and accommodating 500 puncheons (a puncheon is a large cask with a capacity varying between 70 and 120 gallons). This was a gabled building, originally U-shaped, with the 'open' side facing east; between 1824 and 1834 a fourth side was added, forming a hollow square. It is now an hotel and has recently been restored.

68 Shot Hall (Barbados Yacht Club)

In 1824 this was the quarters of the Officer Commanding the Royal Engineers and was described as built of stone, on two floors, measuring 70 ft by 40 ft. It suffered severe damage in the hurricane of 1831. It was part of the package sold in 1906 which included the Engineers' Pier (65) and subsequently became the Barbados Yacht Club.

Barbados Yacht Club (formerly Shot Hall)

69/70/71 *Barrier Bridge, Garrison Wall and Stables*

The Barrier Bridge was built in 1802, over a section of a large pond, to assist the Army in getting its stores up to St. Ann's. It formed the entrance to the Garrison from the Bridgetown direction; the section of Garrison Wall on the east side of the road bears the number WD 6 and extends to the sea at Burke's Beach, where it bears the number WD 1.

Section of the Garrison Wall

72 Garrison Wall (in Banyans Condominium)

In this area there was in 1822 a building described as the residence of the Commanding Officer, Royal Artillery; all that remains is the Wall, in the grounds of what is now the Banyans Condominium.

73 Commissariat Provision Store (Barbados Light and Power Company Headquarters)

Built about 1793–1801, it was designed to accommodate 3500 tierces (one 'tierce' is a 42 gallon cask) of provisions; it is shown in 1824 as the Commissariat Provision Store, on three floors, of stone, measuring 90 ft by 40 ft. It was refitted in 1893 to house the Garrison Theatre (42). It was acquired in 1909 by the Barbados Electric Supply Company, later the Barbados Light and Power Company, which was responsible for its restoration in 1986; it houses the headquarters of the Company.

BUILDINGS OUTSIDE THE GARRISON HISTORIC AREA

Given the situation in Barbados, with the declaration of war by France in 1778, it was inevitable that there should be many military installations in the island, some outside the Garrison area, not forgetting the redoubt under construction in 1779 at Fort George, about two and a half miles east of Bridgetown, but never completed and of which few traces remain. Those buildings associated with the Military Garrison which are most worth a visit are described below.

Medical Pavilion (The Pavilion, at Hastings)

This shell of a building (awaiting restoration) on the north side of the Hastings Road, and known as the Medical Pavilion, was the residence of the Surgeon in charge of the Military Hospital. It was built in 1805 and suffered only slight damage in the hurricane of

1831, and so was used as a temporary hospital for the injured. It passed into private hands in 1908 and was for a time used as a residence before being converted into flats.

Military Hospital (Pavilion Court)

Situated immediately to the east of the Medical Pavilion, these buildings were erected in 1803–1806; they were badly damaged in the 1831 hurricane and not restored until 1840, when they were again in use as a hospital. They were converted into apartments in 1928.

St. Matthias Church

In St. Matthias Gap, off Hastings Road, the foundation stone was laid on 1 August 1837 by William Hart Coleridge, Bishop of Barbados and the Leeward Islands (effectively of the English-speaking Caribbean except for Jamaica) but construction proceeded slowly and, while the unfinished church was licensed and opened for worship in 1841, it was not consecrated until 1850. In the absence of a Garrison chapel (36) it was used by the Garrison forces from 1848.

The church is now used by the Defence Force on official occasions; it has recently been restored.

The Dauntless Memorial

In the grounds of St. Matthias Church, this is a memorial to the officers and men of HMS Dauntless, most of whom died of fever in 1852. It has recently been restored.

Officers of Deputy Adjutant-General and Deputy Quartermaster-General (Old Eye Hospital)

This building, on Bay Street opposite Jemmott's Lane, was built before 1817 when it was purchased for use as the offices of the Deputy Adjutant-General and Deputy Quartermaster-General. It later housed the offices of the Garrison headquarters staff and in 1881 was converted for use as a recreational centre for the Army and Navy, known as the United Services Home. In 1887 it became the Married Quarters for the Adjutant-General's staff and in 1906 was sold to the Barbados Government and used by the General Hospital (then in the buildings in Jemmott's Lane now turned into Government offices) as a ward for pellagra and later eye patients.

It now houses the Welfare Department and has recently been restored with the help of a grant from the Canadian Government.

King's House (now Queen's House)

This building, in Queen's Park, was constructed in 1783 to replace an earlier building and became the residence of the Commanding Officer of the British forces in Barbados and the Windward and Leeward Islands. It included a signal station linked with the system of signal stations across the island set up in the early nineteenth century.

It has been restored in recent years, in part with the help of the late Oliver Messel, and converted into a theatre upstairs and art gallery below.

Deputy Adjutant-General's Residence (The Retreat)

Built prior to 1780 and formerly the residence of the Deputy Adjutant-General this building is now part of the property of Harrison College.

The Lock Hospital (until recently residence of the Sergeant-Major in charge of the Harbour Police)

This building, once a hotel, was converted into a hospital in an attempt to cope with a serious increase in the mid nineteenth century in the incidence of venereal disease, particularly syphilis, among both troops and local inhabitants. In December 1867 the Imperial Government agreed to contribute £2500 toward the 'erection of a hospital capable of affording twenty five Lock-Ward-Beds . . .'. The term 'Lock' was used in the fifteenth century with reference to a leper hospital in Southwark, near London, which became a VD hospital, and was probably so called to indicate isolation or quarantine. The hospital was closed in 1887 and later

Former Lock Hospital

became the residence of the Sergeant-Major in charge of the Harbour Police; it is now used by the Royal Barbados Police Force for the housing of officers.

THE NATIONAL CANNON COLLECTION

Some 30 cannon have been mounted on the Savannah to form the nucleus of the collection. These range from the mid seventeenth century through to the late nineteenth century. The Royal Cyphers of Queen Anne, the three Georges and Queen Victoria are all to be seen. The largest gun on show is the Rifled 7" Muzzle Loader of 1870 and the rarest is the Commonwealth Cannon with Cromwell's Republican Arms on it, one of only two known to exist in the world.

The National Cannon Collection with the Main Guard and the Ordnance Barracks in the background

Cannon showing Cromwell Gun on the far left (there are only two of these in the world)

Outside the central collection approximately one hundred additional guns have been recorded. Some of these are the property of Government and could be made available to the collection, others are privately owned. What is known is that Barbados possesses the largest collection of seventeenth century iron cannon in the world and it is hoped that many of these will find their way eventually into the National Cannon Collection.